This book belongs to:

To Gram for our summer memories at the beach.
-A.M.

Meet July
Text and Illustrations copyright ©2024 by April Martin
Calendar Kids Books, LLC | Kathleen, GA 31047
ISBN: (Paperback) 978-1-957161-19-8, (Hardback) 978-1-957161-20-4
Library of Congress Control Number: 2024908350

To find out more about The Calendar Kids® Collection, visit www.calendarkids.com
and sign up for newsletters or follow us on social media @thecalendarkids.

The Calendar Kids
meet
JULY

POW

BOOM

April Martin

This is July.

July loves sipping on freshly squeezed lemonade. He loves his star-shaped sunglasses. He loves his red-and-white striped swim trunks and blue rash guard too! He loves them so much he wears them to the pool almost every day.

He spends the summer hanging out with his friends, June and August, by the pool. "It's too hot to do anything else outside today," July moans. "It has to be over 100 degrees!"

June, July, and August stay cool by the pool with homemade watermelon ice pops and watermelon slices. July **loves** watermelon!

He eats so... much... watermelon.

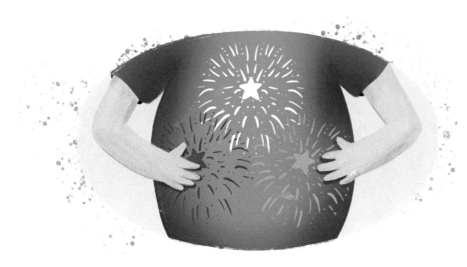

So much, his belly got **rounder** and **rounder**.

He even believed June when she told him he had a watermelon growing in his belly.

GULP!

I think I'm going to faint...

What July doesn't love are the afternoon summer storms that come through his town almost every single day! They are so scary. So loud. So rumbly. July knows he must go inside when he hears thunder rumble.

His mom taught him to seek shelter to stay safe. She reminds him of her rule, "Lightning is dangerous!
July, time to come in!"

"Oh man, we were just headed to the pool again," July groans.

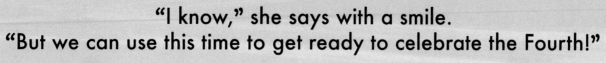

"I know," she says with a smile.
"But we can use this time to get ready to celebrate the Fourth!"

"That's right!
Great idea,
Mom!"
July shouts.

He LOVES to celebrate America's birthday on the fourth of the month. Every year, he enjoys watching different parades with his family. The Fourth is celebrated all over America with fireworks, parades, and barbecues!

One year, his family went to Bristol, Rhode Island, to watch the parade on their red, white, and blue-lined streets. This is America's oldest parade of all! July learned that this parade has been going on for more than 200 years!

Another year July, and his family wanted to watch the parade in Gatlinburg, Tennessee... but they couldn't stay awake. It started in the middle of the night at 12:01 a.m.!

Zzzz...

fireworks...

Zzzz...

hot dogs...

Zzzz...

flags...

This year, July was excited to stay home and enjoy their local town parade. July was even invited to be on one of the parade floats! He had a lot of work to do, so he invited his friends over to help get their float ready for the parade.

June, July, and August worked together to create red, white, and blue banners to decorate their float.

"Ugh! The flies are so bad this summer!" June said. "Do we have any bug spray we can bring to the parade?"

July's pet chameleon, Sizzle, tried to help with bug patrol.

The day of the local parade finally arrived.

Party like it's
1776!

"Happy Fourth," July said to his friends. "Our float looks amazing!"

Everyone in town lined up to watch the parade.
They listened as the band banged their drums.
The trumpets started to play too!

Brrr- br- brrrrrr!

BOOM! BOOM!
BOOM! BOOM!

toot   toot

toot   toot

Rat-a-tat-tat!

July thought he heard another summer thunderstorm on the way but hoped it was just the sounds from the band.

"That is DEFINITELY thunder," July said as he began to worry.
"Our day is ruined! This may be the worst Fourth ever."

July thought he would be sad to see all of their hard work rained out.

"It's getting closer! Shouldn't we all go inside?"

But no one else seemed worried.

"EVERYONE TAKE COVER! Lightning is close!"

But they only stared at him.

"Uh, July, that's just your hair," August giggled.

"Oh! Right! Oops! It does that sometimes."
July blushed.

The parade and fireworks went on as planned. July thought spending this summer in their small town parade with family and friends was an extra special way to celebrate America's birthday this year.

"What will we do now that the celebrations are all over?"
July asked his friends the next morning.

"Cannonball!"

My July Notebook

Special July birthdays or events in my family:

The best part about the month of July is...

July is the seventh month of the year.

July has 31 days.

The month after July is August.

July is a summer month.

If you are born in July, your birthstone is the ruby.

Canada celebrates its birthday this month too! July first is Canada Day!

The Fourth of July, Independence Day, is when we celebrate America becoming its own country. It's America's birthday!

Discussion Questions

1. July stays cool on hot summer days by going to the pool. Name some other ways you can stay cool in the summer.

2. June told July he was growing a watermelon in his belly. Do you think that can really happen? GULP!

3. July has celebrated Independence Day all over America. How do you celebrate the Fourth of July?

4. July's pet chameleon is named Sizzle. What does the word "sizzle" mean?

5. July is afraid of another afternoon storm coming. Why do you think he is so worried?

6. *Crack, bang, pop,* and *boom* are all sounds that you can hear. We call these onomatopoeias. Can you name more words that are sounds we can hear?

Homemade Watermelon Ice Pops

You will need:

2   cups of watermelon, cubed
1/2   cup water
2   tablespoons of honey (or sugar)
1   tablespoon of lime juice
blender
ice pop mold tray (makes 6)

Directions:

1. Ask a grown-up to cut the watermelon in to cubes.

2. Add watermelon, water, honey or sugar, and lime juice to a blender.

3. Blend the ingredients until they look smooth.

4. Pour the mixture into the ice pop trays.

5. Put the tray in the freezer for 4 to 5 hours.

6. Carefully remove the ice pops from the tray and enjoy!

meet APRIL

Author April Martin didn't have a chameleon growing up, but she did have an iguana— she even had leopard geckos in her classroom!

April loved celebrating the Fourth of July on the beach as a child. She stayed cool in the summer by jumping in the Gulf of Mexico near Florida. Now as a grown-up, if she's not outside in her garden, she's either spending time with her children in the pool or inside enjoying the AC.

The Calendar Kids
meet AUGUST
April Martin

The Calendar Kids
meet SEPTEMBER
April Martin

The Calendar Kids
meet OCTOBER
April Martin

To learn more about when the next Calendar Kids® books will be available, visit www.calendarkids.com!

Made in the USA
Las Vegas, NV
25 June 2024

91491829R00026